Chariot

Cha

WAVE BOOKS SEATTLE / NEW YORK

Timothy Donnelly

Published by Wave Books

www.wavepoetry.com

Wave Books titles are distributed to the trade by

Consortium Book Sales and Distribution

Phone: 800-283-3572 / SAN 631-760x

Library of Congress Cataloging-in-Publication Data

Names: Donnelly, Timothy, author.

Title: Chariot / Timothy Donnelly.

Description: First Edition. | Seattle : Wave Books, [2023]

Identifiers: LCCN 2022045041 | ISBN 9781950268818 (hardcover)

ISBN 9781950268771 (paperback)

Subjects: LCGFT: Poetry.

Classification: LCC PS3604.O5637 C43 2023 | DDC 811/.6—dc23/eng/20220926

LC record available at https://lccn.loc.gov/2022045041

Designed by Crisis

Printed in the United States of America

9 8 7 6 5 4 3 2 1

First Edition

Wave Books 108

for Mary Jo Bang

I

II

To be in any form, what is that?

In My Life

I have never seen the Milky Way the way it looks in pictures
    in my feed on Instagram—which is to say like the trail of froth
a sperm whale makes in videos when it swims up close
    to the air, but immeasurably more luminous, and spattered everywhere

in tiny barnacles of stars, whole portions of the sky
    stained improbably azure, purple, teal; a general sense of
superimposition but no real threat of being pounced on or made to suffer
    in captivity, the specter of symphonic music off in the background

of the mind relaxing with neurochemicals any suspicion
    vis-à-vis authenticity or preference to not be made a fool of
except by invitation, telling itself somewhere along the way
    it agreed to go along with everything so long as no one gets hurt—

but I have seen its local counterpart in the residues of industry
    haunting the Gowanus Canal, polycyclic aromatic hydrocarbons
and polychlorinated biphenyls, coal tar wastes and heavy metals
    dazzling the surface of the waterway in galactic shapes in peacock

green, gold, sapphire, and while I have no desire to make pollution
    beautiful or to see it romantically, a voice says that's exactly
what I'm doing, while another whispers down to me from a remove,
    saying I am in my life like a dolphin, like a dolphin trapped in a cove.

Nothing Happened

And then it keeps happening. Like a hole in the middle of
    the memory of a field. The interruption of it spreading, widening
out toward the edges. Or is it that the field, receptive,
    pours itself into it? Like a consummation. The way a fire

can realize by feeding. What knows a thing better than
    what consumed it? Like the deepest active black of this
cast-iron pan. Constant reminder: omen of the stove. The dead
    center of an inhuman eye. Its iris is my living space, my entire life.

And what next? Nothing rested, or it may have tried to.
    But everyone in power kept wanting to keep it, to keep it
going. To stop it from solidifying. They needed it to seep
    its way into everything, everything. They needed it to push

past the filters. To replace the filters. They needed it to take
    the place of everything, and it does. It swallows inconsistencies
the way a snake swallows eggs. I crack an egg into the pan;
    I'll crack another. I felt it was the last. I feel there can be

no more. Nothing laughed. And as it keeps laughing, I remember
    a painting of curtains so lifelike, no one who looked at it didn't feel
some new reality stirring inside them. Just look how the folds
    now are starting to disturb themselves. As if about to catch fire.

Sea Whistle

To say there will be no more suffering with such confidence
    is to set the heart on rolling pins
because it knows such a future is impossible in this world, even if
    we reduce the world's dimensions to those of our life raft.

It isn't clear if it's the confidence or the sentiment itself
    that induces this unsteadiness, but I know it's almost always
things in combination, and that disturbances amplify
    the way waves in a bathtub bounce back and forth from the sides.

While I try to devise an all-purpose counterpoise to this
    mess made of language, your impulse is somehow to point
to chestnuts of the genre instead—and here we are again in the dark
    at sea, the exact opposite of our hoped-for circumstances.

As for the life raft, it's hard to go much further with it than
    Géricault, whose infamous canvas, literally larger than life,
divided Paris—so far from the goal of ideal beauty, but undeniable
    in all other respects, its full array of human suffering

heaped up in the frame in subtle pyramids, extremes of hope
    and anguish, endless points of contrast playing off one another
in the ongoing schoolroom of the sea, whose pedagogy serves
    to whittle the bones of confidence down to thin flutes of suggestion.

Night of the Marigolds

Look how the marigolds in the darkness catch the lamplight
     from inside the apartment and bounce it back to us, warning
that we come to be known by the way we respond to
     what we suffer, which is to say by what we have suffered

and not by what we are. In Delacroix's painting of a horse
     frightened by a storm, the animal summarizes thunderclouds
lit by lightning more than horse, unless there's something
     essential to the horse that's unrecognizable as such until

provoked by force. There have been times I've wondered
     about myself, not knowing what it was compared to what
it might have been, or what it isn't, tumbling it over in my mouth
     like raw stone. After a long night of it, if I take the stone

out of my mouth, what surprises me isn't how smooth it is,
     because I expected it to be smooth, but the fact that I have either
troubled it into the shape of a horse, or else sucked away the not-horse
     that kept it from becoming the object it had always meant to be.

Now we are riding into the night. Marigolds towering over us
     drop their scent in waves. Our breathing slows—the horse and I
are in complete communication. The matter of what we mean
     embeds us like a warm Egyptian loam. There's no disputing it.

Summerhead

The dark mud the initiates scoop up from the river and daub
    onto their bodies dries in the sun to a fine ochre-gray.
It cracks in hexagons like the riverbed in drought, and at the joints
    like the hide of an elephant, which the initiates describe

as a mountain on four columns, an emergence of the earth
    inside which all its secrets recombine, a breathing
compendium—the temple that can move and think and feel.
    Its notable proboscis is both a trumpet and a spout for washing.

When the initiates wash off, it's meant to represent
    victory over the material world, its "succession of errors, painful
wanderings, and long journeys by tortuous ways," Plutarch says—a step
    toward the nonstop meadow they'll enter after death. But when I

take my turn with the hose, I bet I end up loving being in the body
    even more than I did before, and to feel it returned to me
post-estrangement, freed of the mess I'd plastered on by choice—
    the way I sometimes choose walking back and forth in high heat

carrying a parcel—will be like rebirth, like getting to know
    life a second time, here in the cool quiet of a home, unpacking
provisions I had nearly forgotten about—a dozen apricots, this thistly
    flower I can't pronounce, this crackling of cellophane like fire.

Excelsior

I know no single work of architecture should ever be counted on
        to accommodate the whole of what we feel, but the idea
that some structure might do so doesn't just abandon you
        the way a perfume does, suddenly vanishing after holding you up

in a room made of scent. It stays with you, like a barnacle
        you wish for, or like a vision of cholesterol lining your arteries
more vividly than the blood itself. I feel I am the ship
        in all analogies involving ships, and because nothing stops

me from doing what I do, I envision the ship deliberately
        ignoring signs and signals, lunging its prow into the storm,
proving itself against the night rocks—completely cracking apart!
        I didn't say I was the captain; there might be none on board

or a dozen for all I know: I am the ship itself, disintegrating
        into the absolute correctness of the sea
to do as it pleases. But I will say this: even as the storm I chose
        snaps the mast of me in half, which had been the imponderable

trunk of a single conifer, and even as my hull like gingersnaps
        shatters into the fact of the coast, silhouetted by the eventual
lights of the search party—I still can't stop myself, I reach up in hope
        to find a work that will accommodate the whole of what I've felt.

The Light

Isn't it the work of those of us who work to make new tools
    with the tools we are given, hammering matter
into matter more adapted to the hand than to the memory
    of a hand, less to the past than to the path to what comes next?

And isn't it the work of the next adaptation in part to evince
    specifically by being what it is, regardless of detail and whether it
wants to or not, the matter of persistence through change,
    the hammering of being into time, which is itself the work?

And so it was I took myself downriver, early in the midst
    of the worldwide sickness, the light on me knowledgeable
as all light is knowledgeable, silent archive
    of everything that happens—it puts you in your place, the light

put me in my place. Light on the surface of East River in March,
    light July through October, light at noon on slopes of undulations
pearling for a moment till it gleams up on the peaks, the light
    like melon ribbon, light dribbling from the mouth of a mythical

beast like Blake's dragon, but in effect, closer to a nebulous
    walrus made of fire. I am the nebulous walrus made of fire. I walk
among you unrecognized but laughing. There is so much beauty
    left to see in this world. And I became what I am now to see it.

Etruscan Vase with Flowers

If ever a blue could bypass the forebrain and make its appeal
    directly to the amygdala, you are that blue. Hybrid of raincloud
and of periwinkle—not the mollusk, which is thought
    to have been brought to the Americas stuck to the rock

ballast of European trade ships, but the tint of that eponymous
    invasive ground cover whose simple blooms are known elsewhere
as the flower of death, after the ancient custom of placing
    wreaths of them on heads of dead children, or more accurately

at their feet—you leap from the ochres of everything else
    multidimensionally, like a mystic whisper in an ordinary place.
A Staples comes to mind. Strange name, seeming to mean to conjure
    essentials, yet totally overshadowed by the image of metal

fixtures forging connection via puncture and force. You understand
    how vivid specificity kills juice, obviates and thereby
sterilizes the mind's invention. You exist in opposition. You open
    with unreal flowers what the logic of prose means to close through

the hours of my existence, which diminish in number, whereas
    infinity does not. You, wordlessly, argue the feasibility
of transport, the way Redon himself told poets of his day to look
    to the sea, whose only options are unboundedness and boundlessness.

Drift

Hwæt! There was a universe of words and in it I could fly
     sans impediment, no sediment
could muck up the spout of me, what poured out of me
     poured steadily as coconut milk from the can, or like a melody

sung by a solitary shepherdess to prolong her courage
     after sunset in Saxony. She turns to face the cold salt wind
off the rough North Sea and watches day's semicircle
     whittled brighter, more slender. There was a universe around her

and a universe inside her: crescent moon, Venus;
     not so much memories of events
as blueprints of purpose, a feeling that songs can open up spaces
     a life can live inside without growing tired of itself.

I myself had grown tired of myself. True to form, philosophy
     said hours of mountain climbing make strange
comrades of opponents, that tiredness is the shortest path
     to equality and fellowship, and that each of us finds liberty,

eventually, in sleep. And so it was I bore the weight of me up
     an incline as a second person: not expecting to enjoy
ourselves and we didn't, but after, in exhaustion, we lacked the wit
     to quarrel anymore, and in our sleep we built this spaceship.

Elevation

AFTER CHARLES BAUDELAIRE

Over gutters and over parking lots,
    over rooftops, fountains, cloudbanks and the bay,
beyond the sun, beyond the medium that fills
    unoccupied space, beyond the confines of the known

universe, ghost, you slip out of me
    with the ease of a swimmer
at one with the waves, furrowing the deep
    with a pleasure we can't articulate

as we fly from the contagion
    of the world, bathing in vibrations
shed in silence from the stars, drinking up
    the cold clear fire that purifies our emptiness.

Only when you ferry us
    here, beyond the tedium and despair
that weigh us down, can we be happy, only when
    animate wings beat through the haze of life and lift

up into the luminous do our thoughts like birds
    trace patterns in the pearl-gray sky
and hover over life, understanding without effort
    the lexicon of the flowers, the syntax of all that will die.

Where Space Begins

It depends on who you are, and what you're after. If you're NASA
    handing out silver astronaut pins, space starts exactly
fifty miles above the planet. But if you're less scientific than that,
    and want only to find your way through the dark, hands groping

for the word for the banister, space might begin
    at the surface of your skin, or even underneath it. Let's stay
here a moment, pasting it together, listening to weather
    come into its own as it hits an obstruction—rain on the window,

wind on the tarp—words as they loosen
    hold of the world, peeling away from what they can't quite become
in order to be more completely what they are—taking off
    after midnight, like geese do, so the realists can't track them

en route to another level, they set root in what they posit
    apart from what they point to, making a space of themselves
anyone can wander in—a garden without entry fee. I write to you now
    from its hot-pink periphery, about to set foot in the pleasure of it

outright—a maze of azaleas at full tilt, an open-air temple
    built not for worshipping gods in their heights, but right here
among us in clouds of abundance as they recombine
    words whatever way they can, exposing the backend of the possible.

The Yellow Boat

One cannot have too much yellow . . .

—PIERRE BONNARD

The hull of it recalls the sky
    where sunlight strikes the clouds in streaks
like pollen from a lily's mouth
    when suddenly it tumbles onto the cotton tablecloth.

December
    drags a finger through it and it works
its sigil deeper
    into the weave, into the fiber of it, conjugation

of plant with plant, minuscule
    but also cosmic as the solar barque, or like a thought
that races
    between two places, discontent

with disconnection—a honeybee traversing
    air among sunflowers
and as joyous. It spreads its residue of pleasure
    like a message on a breakfast plate, a quickness in

chrysanthemum, thin memento of a hair—
    goldfinch, raincoat, Post-it note
like a winter pasture seen midair, a metaphor
    for life itself, this citrus scent its instrument of power.

Night of the Gowanus

The drum track refers to matter's tendency to integrate
    while the notes that make up the melody assert themselves
as individuals, the way particles constitutive of wholes
    always do, recapitulating the dynamic equilibrium of the universe.

Streams of tail- and headlights on the curve of the viaduct
    outlined like clip art with the peach tones of sunset under it
and above it a sky's ombré of icicle- to coal-blue—where a faint few
    stars think things over—refer to motorists

as iridescent geometrics on the rippling face of the water
    refer to the coal tar dumped into it by industry for
over a century, sludging the canal-bottom in thicknesses equal
    to twenty mattresses piled one on top the other, as in a fairy tale

of sensitivity, except these mattresses are irrevocably toxic,
    and the princess is a phantasm of oyster shells
and auto parts, parts likewise of bodies disappeared here in the dark,
    lives grieved without finality as the canal itself is grieving

the tidal inlet of bright creeks intricate with water life
    it used to be before Dutch settlers perplexed it into property
from the Lenape, humanity again done in by its own traffic,
    confusing its light with stars, to whom such details matter nothing.

Weather Heard as Music

Tonight the great night wind blows hard against the building
    as if we were at sea, as if we were at war
and I some royal personage kept far from care, a softness
    cocooned among the battlements, gold-white worm

floating with ease through the infected air, solemn
    parade, the high-pitched ceiling painted blue
then decked in stars—a shame so many should have to pay
    for my effects, they never last. I must represent

a thing of value. Don't go through with it, don't go
    through with it, but even now I can feel
it is myself who slips away. And there is no great truth
    I stand for, no great meaning. It is only the wind.

And there is no great truth I am serving, only details
    of minor things that befall: cake crumbs on the tabletop,
rubble waiting to be poked through a little further
    before the froth of the wave comes to shuffle it off

into the dark, indescribable deep, where I dissolves
    so unorchestratedly, by the time it all unfolds
into some new form of life, it has long since washed ashore
    like a family member, hovered over until recognized.

Angel of the Hearth

When it came it was like a cherry popsicle
    melting down the arm of a stranger's child, colorful
and sloppy, but having nothing to do with you, you could walk past it
    on the crosswalk and not think twice. Or when it came

it was like a festival
    of some religious intent, the wax effigy of a saint
confused in flowers out of season shedding blessings down your street
    with amateur music on a litter built by hand by the avid.

Or when it came it was like the avid
    hands of strangers pulling knobs and switches, leaving
traces in the air's clear wax like litter you have shed like music
    without intent in the course of your developed day. Or like the spirit

inhabiting a neighbor, one who grabs you by the arm
    for balance on the crosswalk and quick
as math you feel the power isn't where you expect it, it can hide
    anywhere it decides, and nothing will go right for you for weeks after,

months—keys will go missing, money
    won't reach you, new milk sours in the fridge overnight—
and as you sit at your hearth for comfort, it will be there in that fire
    caressing you, erasing you, filling you with images of things you'd kill for.

No Small Task

Make dust our paper and the ink will be our tears and to write
 will be to stand there remembering, sorrowfully remembering
the days, the weeks, the years, which is an adaptation
 of the second Richard, whose metaphors were inclined to divorce

notions like the truth and spirit and one's wishes from the clodgy
 mucky rocky solids of our planet, pulverized and shed
habitually into the dust we stand writing into, and when finished
 we watch the winds erase our progress, which was no progress at all

but stasis in a double sense, which is because we stood there
 as we poured our little tribute out, but also because it stood for
our having done so, a kind of monument like the wavy
 traces a snake makes under the right circumstances, which include

the snake itself (a given), sand in quantity, time, the volition of
 the snake to move through space, which is also to move
through time, and lastly the capacity of the snake to do so, meaning
 the absence of hindrances intrinsic to the snake or otherwise in play.

No small task! And yet the number of snakes at present writing
 movement from here to there, both specifically and as an example
of beauty to be found in phenomena, proves equally uncountable
 as sand in quantity, waves in water, waves likewise through the air.

Night of Embodiment

I feel differently about my fingers when I think of them as fringes
    at the end of my arms than I do when I remember them
as distinct appendages extending independently from my hands.
    It's hard to describe the difference, but something in me

says I have to, and it's something I obey. There's a kind of bookmark,
    very simple—a strap of leather, genuine, nine inches long,
two inches wide (measurements will vary), and the bottom
    knuckle-length or so is slit several times vertically to make

the kind of fringe I'm thinking about. But by the time I express it
    this way, another noses into life like purply tentacles
tasseling the sleeve-like body of a squid, itself an offshoot
    of the first idea, and then the Nile Delta, which feels like a whole

new thing, but nothing about the Nile is new, not the stars
    above it and not papyrus tilting up out of its bed toward Gemini
to birth our word for paper, its stalks exploding at their termini
    into emerald-tree-frog thread-like rays, yet another example of right

back where we started. But if we cut one stalk into a stylus and slice
    the rest into strips we soak, weave, and submit to pressure,
we can express the ink from our squids' ink sacs, plus that mystic
    touch of it behind the eyes, and document our travels for the future.

Honeymouth

As Pindar slept at the foot of Mount Helicon, a swarm of bees
    assembled a honeycomb in the crevice of the poet's open mouth.
That's what I'm talking about. The substance of the planet
    may be finite, but its permutations are limitless. Remember

to give thanks for this. Remember everything that happened, even
    twenty-six centuries ago, might be happening again
right now. And so it was I walked out into the snow. I needed to feel
    free to mix with the stuff of reality in ways I hadn't planned.

I needed to let the voice of middle management
    asking me why I want to make things difficult slide from
my brain and back into the abyss. When compromise seeks to maximize
    profit, its logic is corporate—if not in the strict sense, then at least

metaphorically. To feel what is right, to look into your heart
    and know it, but to find yourself in a microclimate that refuses
that validity, that demonizes you for holding on to it rather than giving
    in and going with the flow—which is the current of corporate

power protecting corporate power—is the nightmare Pindar
    woke from, mouth stoppered with honey and wax. I want to make
things difficult like that, gumming up the works midflow, so when Apollo
    arcs his chariot toward night, in my speechlessness I'll learn to sing.

Myth

AFTER LADY GREGORY

Like a thought a person tries not to be pursued by, the hunting party
 approached midnight—the purple mountain! A dozen bipeds
accompanied by quadrupeds in two size categories: a smaller
 and a larger. On the backs of the larger, the bipeds sat, mounted.

In no time, a third kind of quadruped charged forth! Midsize,
 but outfitted with warlike appurtenances and fuming
at the nostrils, it attacked the smaller quadrupeds, slaughtering half
 and leaving many others wounded. The bipeds, increasingly

human, moved to retaliate—but a tall shadow stepped out from
 a crack in the mountain, explaining that the midsize quadruped
was in fact his beautiful daughter, as she now appeared to be.
 Thankful to the hunters for sparing his child, the shadow king

invited them into his palace—vivid red, a raftered ceiling
 like a chest cavity. Everyone partook in the human pastimes:
food and drink, competitive mummery, aimless conversations like vines
 spun around the animals outdoors. Above all, the singing

of the princess, who drew our attention to a harp of three strings:
 an iron string, which made whoever heard it cry; a bronze,
that made the listener laugh; then a silver, which carried us to sleep.
 Waking, we find ourselves outside again, upright among the animals.

Complicity

I have made myself at home in this crumbling
    world of empire, adhering to it like a shipworm
pioneer to the wooden belly of a vessel up to something
    questionable no doubt. The voyages of humanity

always have to do with money, and by voyages
    I mean movement of any sort. Even our most poetic conversations
fall like veiled sales pitches; all our sales pitches play
    like conversations with our armpit: greed, brutality, fear;

ignorance and so forth. The point is to trick
    one another into feeding on whatever makes us feel
hungry all the time. The mollusk's larvae will affix
    themselves to any wood submerged in seawater, and there

they grow their long, pale, vermicular bodies and the tiny
    helmet-like shells they use to bore the tunnels
they live their lives out in, cultivating in their gills bacteria
    whose enzymes break wood down into a digestible substrate.

Ships, riddled, sank. England, however, rich in copper,
    sheathed her hulls with it to halt the shipworm's progress,
and as a bonus, the metal reduced the fleet's resistance in water—
    leaving it not only worm-safe, but faster, sleeker, dominant, unstoppable.

All Vanishes

AFTER COMTE DE LAUTRÉAMONT

Old ocean, salty bachelor, when you roam
    the solitude of your realm, you are right to
grow boastful over the magnificence of what you are
    and give birth to, plus all that love you get from poets!

Voluptuously balanced by the soft perfume
    of your imperturbable slowness,
the most grandiose among the attributes
    circumstance has bestowed on you, you unroll—

emboldened by your own ambiguity, and over the whole
    of your surface—waves in cursive, demonstrating a steady
propensity for endlessness. Each hastens after the other
    in parallel, individuated by an interval, a glimmer—no sooner

does one dissolve than the next rises up to meet it
    where it dies, accompanied by the melancholy tone
of the foam as it melts into air, warning us that all is foam,
    all vanishes, even the migratory bird

that rests on you with confidence, entrusting its body
    to the movements of your body, proud
echo of your finesse, until the bones of its wings
    recover, and are strong enough now to resume their flight.

Eau de Nil

From the treadmill through the window overlooking the scrapyard
     I watch twin cranes—bright yellow, outfitted
with grapples—pick up their heap-sized pinches of scrap
     and tenderly convey them from one mountain of it to the next.

There's a logic to it I don't watch closely enough to detect
     but nonetheless trust exists. Sometimes when the machines
face each other, their angularly arched arms
     cross, forming the iconic golden M of McDonald's, and there's

a McDonald's a three-minute walk from here, but I've only
     visited it once throughout the worldwide sickness
and that was last March to buy my daughters the infamous
     seasonal mint-green shakes. Their color, if remarkable, literally

can't hold a candle to the surface of the Gowanus
     when it reflects the two nearby drum-like light vivid green
silos I assume pertain somehow to the scrapyard, possibly to store
     more ruin than the human eye can bear, which turns out

to be a lot. I think of lost friends; I think of lost opportunities; I try
     my best to think of nothing. This is life, absolutely
and without distinction, such that even if I wanted to discern
     the face that's wet from sweat from one that's crying, I could not.

Domesticity

Under the castor bean plant, tall as a giraffe, I imagined my life
    felled by the toxins. Absorbing a bitter monograph
between cold lentils and a long hot bath, I wished its author
    felled by the toxins. Australopithecus, small-brained and largely

fructivorous, may well have been felled by the toxins, but we
    have stamina. We were built to last. Look at that
shooting star—shit, you missed it. Look at this picture of
    charcuterie—I'll forward it. Look what happened to the rue—

I overwatered it. I need to check the drainage holes and
    just leave it be. I need to hold life close to me. I need to wash it
by hand, even if it's dishwasher-safe. We need to keep it away
    from all these animals. What happened before can't happen again.

Slathering the butter on, I wondered who eats the most butter.
    Hauling garbage down to the garbage area, I wondered
who eats the most garbage. Responding apologetically to the messages
    requesting hours of my lifeforce, I wondered how much longer

before function distorts the medium completely. Before the terminal
    dram is squeezed out of me. Before I wake to an afterlife
all in white, like the rest of the waitstaff. Before I look to the time
    and can't make out its face, or can't remember what the word is for.

Nocturne

There never was an Art-loving nation.

—JAMES MCNEILL WHISTLER

Midnight at the pit of my irrelevance:
    a hair's breadth away, I step closer to the mouth of it, no more afraid to
shake hands with my lacuna than a bird is of the air
      whistling in its bones. To stay possible as long as possible

had felt like enough now—a persistence of streaks
    in soft butter yellow shed from the clock tower onto the indigo-
freaked slate-to-black vagueness
      that indicates the river. The light lives

on like this, drowning by day
    in its own muchness, sensed most acutely at night
where there's less of it, when its difference from what dominates
      sharpens its edges, or the perception of its edges, so that its presence

is felt
    contradistinctively—not a thing of the world, but against it
and inside you, less parasite than language
      awakening the vacancy, fluorescing what it means, its marks on the page

of the water a welcome, a widening
    outside yourself and into a manifold that can't be marketed
or observed, so if anyone's near you when it happens, they won't know
      what's happening—they won't know you're more than what you answer to.

Not Much More to It Than That

One thing hides another. Thing A can't hide without Thing B
    to hide behind, or in, or under. And when it hides it must be hiding
from a third. Everything is hiding in some regard, if only you
    can find it. Take your time. If things were easy, wouldn't that

defeat the purpose? The purpose is to make things hard, lasting,
    and beautiful to see. Sunset is gorgeous, but it doesn't last. That the sun
sinks under the horizon is the cause, that it hides there is the cost
    of all that beauty. If this presents a moral quandary, remember we

are merely its onlookers. An onlooker is a form of Thing C
    against which the efforts of Thing A are failing, in spite of itself
or on purpose. To fail on purpose is a form of beauty that leaves
    the onlooker reassured—we see what's happening right in front of us,

albeit after a pause. The bird sickens, the roof collapses, the sun
    declines, failing to remain overhead. Even our words as we cross
one last time, here in this ill-suited cabin—what with the banging
    and rapidly decreasing oxygen level—are hiding and failing to hide,

which proves a comfort in our hour of need. Plus it's beautiful to see
    things fall to pieces as they intend to, or even as they must,
so long as you've prepared yourself—eyes open, gloves off; one hand
    placed firmly in the other, the other placed firmly in a third, and so forth.

Night of Oblivion

Enigmatic purple on a plate of crumbled cloud, the dot at the center
    of the wildflower Queen Anne's lace is said to recall a drop
of Stuart blood pricked onto a doily the queen was at work on
    when something distracted her from her purpose. History forgot

to document what broke the queen's focus, but it seems to me
    fairly obvious, having lived with it long enough, that memory
was the culprit. "You again," she gasped, pivoting her face
    forty-five degrees to appeal directly to the bright sun to prise

unwelcome remembrance from the countless fast raccoon hands of
    her neurons. Strong sensation obliviates thought, thus
this preponderance of neighborhood leaf blowers, synecdochic
    of much of Western culture. It takes so much loudness to remove

an oak leaf from a gutter. Native to Afghanistan, the wildflower
    also answers to the name of wild carrot, for no reason other than
that's what it is—its spindly ivory taproot bred over centuries
    into what's become the most reliable source of true hot orange

in most our lives, with the exception of the sun as it sets, which Anne
    took note of in the windows at Kensington Palace, waiting
for pure darkness, the garden only in outline, the ghost of her son
    luminous in moonlight as a paper boat afloat on the still round pond.

Vantablack

Wanting my mind to be quiet as a child, I wondered if a thought
    could survive without words, which always came along
with sound, with noise, even when unspoken, and so I set out to stop—
    surveilling the room from the raft of the bed—my eyes briefly,

wordlessly, when they landed on red—stop sign corkboard, *Merriam-*
    Webster's, stripes on the flag atop *Old Ironsides*—and even as I
sensed this wasn't actual thinking, I was certain at the time
    what I was making, stringing reds together, was a sentence.

Night falls; night falls again, harder; night falls a third time, into the forest
    and the trees trap it there, batting it back and forth
like cats at play with a cockroach, confusing it in its injury
    till it transforms into energy, into the heat that feeds the night

and keeps it restless, an endless circuit like a fountain of crude
    no light can escape from, falling deeper into the spread of itself
forever—but there are no words for what it does; it is the space
    at the mind's molten core where there are no words, there can be

no sound, no noise; the aberration of language only takes place
    outside its borders, our babble skitters off in fear of it like goats
down the face of Mount Etna before an eruption, or before the gasp as I
    sense what I made of red wasn't just a sentence: it was an invitation.

Eglantine

AFTER MARCELINE DESBORDES-VALMORE

Thorn-blossom! Tender thing, prone to solitude
    like yours truly, don't get it twisted if I reach out my hand—
it isn't to pluck you, who are my beacon down this path, but a gesture
    of acknowledgment common among my kind.

When the lukewarm breezes nod off in late shade,
    when the tired day shuts its flaming eyes,
when night's contagion spreads, darkening the leaves,
    it is the light of your perfume that guides me on.

That said, your forehead, dampened in the twilight dew,
    bends down in its burden as if to hide tears;
your perfumes enclose themselves in their white apartment,
    and darkness does unflattering things to your shape and color.

Dog rose, pull yourself together! The day will soon appear
    to reopen your chalice with reanimated fires,
and restore to brightness your dead, or dying, aura.
    That forehead of yours will resume its balmy sparkle!

Meanwhile, myself a stranger to this benightment
    no less than you, I too retreat, surrendering to what
surrounds us; but a beam of hope drills down through the dark as if
    sent from a home planet, and all I have to do for it is wait.

Likely Story

As if a programmed assassin, I won't know how to explain myself
    until it's over, and when it's over, what will be the point
of trying to explain? No one's even here. Some rooms you have to enter
    totally alone, so dark and cavernously new you have no sense

of where the ceiling is, and so you grow close to the floor
    and feel it knows you, feel it feels your thoughts as they rush
through you and into the language center of your brain, where it stands
    upright among decades of curtains, smiling in the delivery room

for the ongoing birth of yourself, which is about as close
    as you can imagine—much closer than you ever had in mind,
but you can't reverse it now. You're in the woods as a child, and look—
    it's suppertime and you've lost your way back! The floor

watches over you, ready to forgive. There must be housekeeping
    I've fallen behind on though, a little tidying up I might do
to make the time more pleasant for us both, but my vision falls short
    of that scene of my truest self, where the mess of it all starts adding up

if only to topple when it's over: bullet to the head, my mission failed.
    Nevertheless, I am pulling together this beautiful confession
to whisper, in the final seconds, to the bug on the carpet, weaving it
    out of words for you at last, you who put me up to it in the first place.

The Gist of It

I could tell they were up to something, the figures in the field,
    by the character of their movements, which bore resemblance to
without exactly replicating each other. If one raised its arms
    into crisp air, another might plunge its hands into the soft earth

while a third and fourth would go about it laterally, one slowly
    and the other in a kind of corresponding frenzy. It drew attention
without sounding alarm. This pattern, if you can call it that,
    repeated throughout the afternoon as a small crowd gathered

on the overhang, mesmerized by the enigmatic undertaking
    the point of which none of us knew or felt we could figure out
based on the information at hand, here on our tartan blankets
    with cheese and wine, a whole array of things brought from home.

A number of us wondered if it served some instructive purpose,
    while others seemed happier likening it to a pure form of dance
that proves its own music. A third felt it had to lie somewhere
    in between, folding elements of both into an interplay that was open

but not aimless, or else why would there be uniforms, when a voice
    said maybe those weren't uniforms so much as garments
cut from the same cloth . . . Only later, after dark, did we stumble
    onto the gist of it, which had been staring us right in the face all along.

Night of the MacGuffin

The George I see in paintings fights a different type of dragon
    than the one I have in mind, which is a tougher-to-pin-down kind
conceptually I think than the typical outsized lizard or snake
    pimped out with one or more of the following: wings, horns,

classic breath of fire, spellcasting capacities, cold glances
    in the style of the basilisk, narcissism (look it up), idiopathic
sleeping habits, fiscal conservatism, troglophilia, high IQ
    and language use, to cite just a few from the long running list

of attributes we commonly ascribe to dragons. The running list itself
    might also be a dragon, self-protracting into the future
of what it refers to, scrolling around the very idea until the mind
    admits defeat in an audible sigh as we continue doing what we do

to get to the next point and the next. Don't look so perplexed
    I say to myself en route to avoid the dragon, which is the only
surefire way to face it, as with a mirror walking backwards into its den,
    so what reaches you isn't magic but a defanged copy of magic,

and this levels the field a bit, seeing what was once so fearful reduced
    to a piss-trickle of images, which sources say is still a post
with power tied to it, but if there's anything I know after all this
    typing, it's the difference between dragons and whatever this thing is.

The Cows

A green this self-evident doesn't need to be addressed bluntly
    to provoke response. Not without its secrets, it is itself
the bluntness, and therefore wants a more roundabout approach
    to reveal its full nature, the way a cow might lift its face up

into a breeze to catch it. Not because it snorts notes of clover unrolling
    yummily in the current's staves, but for the sheer tactility of it.
Afterwards, it can be a challenge to picture cows
    among objects as ponderous as cows themselves, bodily

speaking, with typical examples being Volkswagens,
    Christmas trees, and the leather couches of suburbia.
It might also be unpardonable to set a cow beside such furniture
    in light of its fabrication. Take this as an excuse

to reevaluate chartreuse—with the likelihood of full surrender
    rising with atmospheric pressure. There is no feel
for death here at the moment, no storm, only the cumbersome
    business of life, which must be celebrated. Even if much happens

only to be forgotten, or has happened that we would rather forget,
    still the early morning air clambers up and over and
around things, like a speculative animal that gets to prove itself
    against the shrubbery, garbage, and dormant cars of the street.

Ultramarine

But in a sense I am always looking over a cliff
    overlooking the sea, the thoughts batted out of me in pages
by appointment by the wind, a student of the hazardous
    rhapsody water makes as it slaps against the rocks and into air.

I don't care here that I should be raking in the big bucks,
    working the circuit, peddling the self. I'm too busy breathing
in the ancient fragrance of the sea like the sick cologne a friend gave me
    that smells like church walked into church.

Nor am I impressed anymore by those spiritualistic tricks
    the hustlers pursue to imbue what they do with a shimmer
of significance when what's underneath it all is nothing,
    which is not to be confused with nothingness, which is sacred.

Yves Klein said he signed his name to the sky to make
    his greatest work of art, but look again—that's not his name,
but the French for "Help, I'm bored." And of course he was. Anyone
    with an appetite for the absolute is either overexcitable or

perilously bored, which brings us back to the cliff, the waves
    a true ultramarine, literally "beyond the sea," like Klein's own
patented shade of blue, to which I remain ever-faithful, its value
    equal to a loud prayer that answers itself softly, but also vice versa.

Head of Orpheus

When it was time for the suffering to end, we powered down
    and sat on the steps as if waiting for a chariot
drawn by a loss for words. If only the mind were made to reflect
    the world more completely, as if we agreed to it, we would be free

of so many difficulties—the path ahead of us miraculously
    wrinkleless, cleared of fallen things. What we saw or heard or felt
would be an echo of what was, a duplicate of the present
    willow traced by the sun on the fishpond of our wakefulness.

Easier said than done! Turns out the friction
    between what's real and my take on it might be the battery
that keeps me awake to begin with, and I hadn't stopped to consider
    what happens when we sleep—all those fudgy distortions

and embellishments tricked in gold. This only goes to show
    how scatterbrained hope makes me, how poorly we navigate
when we don't look back to balance what's ahead of us
    against what's behind—fair analogue to what's outside us versus in.

You have less to say at this pivot point than I imagined, or maybe
    you're just keeping it all to yourself for now, but know
as I go on detangling these lines from the invisible, it's always you
    I'm reaching out for, even more so now I can't see where you've gone.

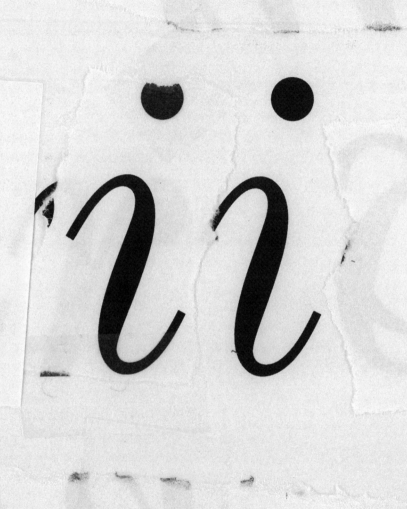

The Bard of Armagh

I have aspired to the ease of the drink-steadied harper
    who lives the tune so thoroughly his fast pink hands
dance over the strings like some sharp thing made sharper
    when it's put to use—a family of thing I can't seem to land

on any member of at present, but its heraldic emblem
    pinned behind me like a charm would be the gold cat's paw
chopping cabbage for the supper I'm forever assembling
    on a field of green to set before the Bard of Armagh.

How I love to drift off as I did all through boyhood
    into the daze of my birthright as a person, even if back then
this inwardness felt like thieving liverwurst sandwiches one should
    leave on the platter for the hardworking women, the men

who need all the more to be propped up on the shillelagh
    of animal protein. I myself was satisfied reclining on the straw
I share a name with all afternoon, festooned in the Boyne Valley
    of self-tillage, grazing millennia with the Bard of Armagh.

The sun hums me awake again! Life is over half over.
    Spent in deference, as ever, to those with much more than me.
One can feed their grief or one can cook up ways to cover
    lack over with graciousness. Neither way will set you free

but one will keep you safer put. Death won't embrace me
    frowning, or it might—but I heard a tune today, and felt an awe
only we who drift far from shore can, a beauty as if meant to save me
    in the currach of its moment, rowed by the Bard of Armagh.

A Page from the Weather

I might take a page from the weather. It pays no attention to the age
    of criticism, age of anxiety, the information age, and so on.
It has nothing to say about the wallpaper. It doesn't care
    what we dip into our fountains of chocolate, if it's angel food

or if it's pound cake, which does tend to crumble too easily.
    In the eyes of the weather, all things partake in this crumbling
tendency; it's only a matter of time, which is also weather
    in an abstract sense, as demonstrated by speakers of French

the whole world over, which is nothing less than weather's
    home and office. We are its prowlers in this sense, interlopers
of a space we can lay no claim to that weather will recognize,
    but to escape would be too painful, or impossible, or expensive,

as proven in the news and deep down in the heart, where feelings
    change and originate. I felt the sun on my back and heard the surf
behind me in my ears. I knew there was nothing I could stop
    the weather from doing. And this is what it means to be alive

in a foreign place, which is everywhere, with the exception of
    these sentences, which make their own weather out of inquiring
what is the nature of our construction, what is the purpose that drives us
    where we go, and how is it possible we live, die, and are born?

Boom

Lotus in the millpond are an image of composition, like swans
    or some comparable waterfowl with long thin neck
and propensity for reflection, or for what passes as reflection but is
    unburdened of its object. There is a stillness and a motion

all at once. They are a gift from heaven. They reverberate
    with presence like periscoping showerheads in mantis green
or fluffy pink eyeballs suspended midflight. They are a laugh
    provoked not by vanity or mockery but happiness in light, as if

against all likelihood. Even the air is moving up
    around these flowers which—anchored in the muck and wriggling
on snakelike stalks amid leaves like floating platters the size
    of manhole covers—act as subwoofers in a system

wired to someplace endless, someplace sheerer than this ghost
    of a reservoir that fed the waterwheel that powered the iron mill
long since converted into condos. The lotus boom the low frequencies
    that recruit large pools of neurons in the listener to lock

the brain into another rhythm, which is to say that they relieve one
    of oneself. It's hard to account for but easy to fathom,
which derives from the Old English for the length of outstretched arms,
    so that to take the measure of a thing is also simply to embrace it.

Beauport

To wax a brick floor, pour a small amount of wax
    in the middle of a four-by-four-foot portion of the floor
and buff it with a mechanized buffer outfitted with a heavy-duty pad.
    Continue applying and buffing wax like this in squares until

the floor is finished. This floor is finished; these ceilings
    low; and temporal vibrations complicate the airspace like the lines
decorating the Nailsea glass, pulled and combed repeatedly
    for that feathery effect, the pattern on it not unlike the harbor's

choppy surface bouncing evening sunlight through the dozens
    of clear panels in the arabesque but simple window of the Master
Mariner's Room, whose floor is made of wide pine planks as if
    a vessel set in motion by the wind. The word *whim* may derive from

the Old Norse for "to let the eyes wander," and that's
    what they do: charts, sextants, compasses; polished whalebone
pointers; books of all description, including a sort of scrollable tablet
    I'd meant to look at more closely but didn't; framed prints

in a child's style; a shelf of decoys, tin soldiers, and what might be
    a bronze coelacanth all lined up as in a class portrait, or like a troupe
rehearsing in a space constructed in hopes that the sea captains of Gloucester
    would want to hold their meetings here, but they weren't interested.

What It Is About People

Actually I think I already get this on a gut level so maybe I shouldn't
    waste anyone's time or memory trying to pin it down.
Even the first steps in that direction, more or less like walking
    into the shopping malls of my youth, quickly render clear

our basic wrongheadedness—you can't grasp the essence
    by purchasing a few particulars, you have to soak in the whole
over time. Record Town, Orange Julius, the palpable not-
    quite-rightness of Spencer Gifts, the luxurious masculine

paisleys of Ralph Lauren. I pointlessly cathect
    onto obsolescing candies at CVS, while in their vividness,
the pieces distract from what they share—the very underneath it
    of it all. "Each of us," said the cashier, although only

in recollection, "is a negligible segment, a quarter inch
    at best, in the national digestive tract, which is measured
in light-years." Still, it's hard to be upset under a ceiling this immaculate
    Marian blue, so unlike the skies of Armageddon, which custom

casts as lurid gray and crumbling, and everyone is running
    to the mall to take shelter, which sounds like a great idea at first,
but habits soon exhaust resources, and the firearms have fallen
    into the wrong hands, and literally no one picks up after themselves!

Home at Last

Tilting my head into the general disorder our present day
    appears to have emerged from
once again without really trying, which isn't exactly the same thing
    as effortlessly, I feel the incalculable factors that underlie

day's structure the way the back of the insomniac must feel
    the box spring, which isn't exactly
the same thing as feeling, but more like extrapolating
    out from what you can feel into places where you can't.

I know this isn't knowing. I know it's more akin
    to making room for a houseguest likely never to arrive.
But if I think of a place I've set foot in only once, or in a dream,
    I still sense the weight of its door, life ringing in the air,

bright rows of packaged goods exclaiming their appeal, and you
    see how I'm already there, reaching for
one thing over another, piecing together a solid plan, holding fast
    to what's holding me up or else laughing it off, even though

I don't yet understand it myself, or how it is I stood
    on the sidewalk just seconds ago, and now I'm down on my knees
on the welcome mat, lit penlight in my mouth like a burglar
    picking his own locked door, in love with the tools of our trade.

Digging for Apples

Give me my shovel
 of love for the sound
it makes slipping into
 the gravelly ground where we buried all the golden ones;

give me my boots
 with weights in the heels
to root me where I am
 and not wanking off in fields of rareripes and dandelions;

give me a backdrop
 of what can't be controlled
to lend me by contrast
 an air of deliberateness, and I'll get back to business, but first—

what if the poem itself
 is what's narcissistic, irrespective
of authorship, and this is
 what makes it appeal to us, not because it can love us but

because it needs us to watch
 it love being
itself, and the surplus we're left with in
 the end is what we call beautiful, like starlight on snowfall?

Air After Fireworks

A squirrel, startled, sets out across the street in successive little leaps
    like the scalloped edging in front-yard gardens used to divide
flowerbeds from the lawn, or like the rim of a glass pie plate
    and then of the pie itself, blueberry, its top crust like a clock face

browning in the oven. Likewise, the squirrel's leaping pattern
    recalls the seconds, minutes, and the hours, which have thus far
proved interminable. Measurements like these, which organize
    one's experience of time and space—including inches, Tuesdays,

summers, decibels, and milligrams—differ from pure mathematics,
    which expresses itself through the physical but exists
prior to expression and so independent of it. This differs, too, from how
    my thoughts on squirrels, fireworks, sicknesses, and pie exist—

to wit, with a haze-like pliancy that almost feels like liberty
    from the spatiotemporal, but without objects to refer to, with no
initial gasp at vibrant suddenness or past captivation by aromas
    arrowing in my direction in a diagram of the kitchen, all my concepts

disappear, and I'm walking home from the drugstore not knowing
    what's happening, what anything is anymore, or where my person
begins, ends, and why it has to be absorbed like a berry into a pie,
    or a squirrel into thoughts of squirrels, night into this fistful of thistle.

Mauled by Dogs

I don't think I'll be mauled by dogs. Time for that has come
    and gone. Time is kept with gears and cogs. Dogs are kept
on chains and leashes. Lashes protect the eye from debris
    and warn it when an object approaches. Ces mots prochains

sont en français. Saying it has made it so. I sometimes fear
    what just can't be. But I don't think I'll be mauled by dogs.
I don't think I can face the world. I wouldn't know what mask to wear.
    Couldn't tell what tree to mark. I went about my so-called work

but couldn't see what for, what for. There seemed to be a mind
    in charge. A hand that fed me scraps of meat. Little drops of garnet
hope is redder than we thought, we thought. A life can't live on life like that
    not knowing it too might be torn apart, but I still don't think

I'll be mauled by dogs—though neither did that bad doctor father
    at the end of *Eyes Without a Face*, who falls face-first
sur la petite colline au bord du bois éclairé doucement au clair de lune,
    when his daughter, masked, sets long-tormented canine subjects

free to pursue their vengeance as she herself finds freedom
    from the cycle of ineffective experimental surgeries to restore
lost beauty, preferring a doe-like difference instead as she steps out into
    the cooler lunar module of the colorless abstract outskirts of Paris.

Reality Hit Me

So I hit back. Bare-knuckled, all my weight, across the ugly
    truth of it. Afterwards, a hand
stings for decades in embarrassment. This impedes one's growing closer
    to the feel of things as they are, making everyday merchandise

hard to hold without a wince. The fight goes on like this
    between oneself indefinitely. But if we have it in our heads
to hit escape velocity, we can't let reality
    do what it wants. We can't just let it swing its clock against our backs

when what we're reaching for is orbit. Cash poor once and sorely
    unimpressed, it was not enough to shoplift
the fine hazelnut chocolate. I had to unwrap it at checkout and pop it
    in my mouth unpaid-for as I looked the shop clerk in the eye.

Time passes and terms self-modify, so I don't know what subtype
    of victory this was, but it felt like saying no to everything
except that chocolate. In the literature, this is known as brutal focus.
    To focus brutally on an object induces a short-lived airlift out of flow

and into the hand of god. Not a hand in the literal sense, or not
    anymore, the hand of god is a pause between breaths you occupy
the way late sunlight harbors ginger in the window, reverberating tint until
    reality hits harder than before, and calls you to account.

Instagram

What if I was uttered into existence through the teamwork of cultists
    and not, as I take it, born of a human woman
under standard conditions: songbirds affirmative, war flickering
    apart on television, rhubarb raising its arms up from the patch?

Would I catch any difference between memories implanted
    into me only yesterday, or whenever it was I was
spanked into action, and those I picked up over time like a janitor
    inching his push broom of consciousness into winter in Wisconsin?

Reality, he thinks, has holes in it, and another oozes through
    like spaetzle from a spaetzle maker, little sparrows of dough
canoodling in the pot's hot storm, skimmed up gently
    and tossed in a bowl with butter, cheese, and caramelized onion.

But it is likewise the soil, the wheat, the clay, and the spinning;
    the grass in the mouth of a cow, the secretion; delayed shipments,
sunsets, and rainfall on advertisements; the unprotected labor
    and Christmas bonuses; every substance and action prior to, after, during . . .

Eat, they say. You have been kept too hungry. What is set in front of you
    is. The road was long due to technical issues but together
we will triumph. Photograph your food. Let everyone you know
    know you know now what your meal is; you know now what's real.

The Material World

The properties, the causes, the evidence, the aromas.
    What wafted up off the forest floor and what glues itself
together by chance. What roots midair. What stops midsentence!
    fills the dank gymnasium stair when management props

open the door in the heat with a trash bin. Tree bark, leaf mold, the oils
    off fallen needles. Certain mushrooms send light signals
the way scorpions and jellyfish do. An eerie green glow
    attractive to arthropods, whose visits hasten spore dispersal.

I know this for a fact: the alternating white and black
    rings on a ring-tailed lemur's tail, thirteen of each, are there
on purpose. Night's overcoat of messages. What cakes up the intake
    valves and sputtering. What fights against its automation

briefly, like a planet. Daylight caught in the baleen of its pixels.
    Skeins of code, suspension cables. What feels the bridge
seaming when it walks it. A walk in the plural. The placedness of
    everything repeated. The stark markings help them to communicate

through their vanishing habitat, where flood tides of merchandise
    mesmerize the workforce, who can't make out what danger
they're electing. Omens come in three. Three or more lemurs make
    a conspiracy. To conspire is to breathe with. A pattern strikes the eye.

Night of the Earworm

Vermis aurium, weirdness emporium, imp orbit orphanage, ora pro
    verbiage; badinage, bandage; bâtonnage, bandwidth;
widdershins, shin splints: beef tongue sandwich. Molecular modicum,
    shopaholic golf cart; modified cornstarch, modesty prevents us

autumn in Modesto, best of the rest home, destination porkchop,
    west-facing parking lot, white-knuckle popsicle: there were nights
when the wind was so cold. Copper mine catastrophe, catfish
    supper club, Tupperware sarcophagus, staphylococcus, a vernacular

for Dracula, crepe-paper ranunculus, Knights of Columbus, rites
    on my rhombus, late fees for services, rendered goose fat, celadon
cachepot, watercolor porticoes, embargoes on whatnot, ultimate
    cinnamon, primrose, bandicoot, butter pat, butter pat, that my body

froze in bed! Voice in a juice box, auditory hopscotch, dishcloth
    whip-poor-will, omen via aerial, malo vocalismo—if I just listened to it
right outside the window. Sic semper vatibus, lapdance applesauce,
    guillotine, goat spleen, pasta fazool. There were days when the sun

was so cruel (terminal universe, bitterest incubus) that all the tears
    turned to dust, debt, the dead, magnetic tape, slow apocalyptic tics
of the face, and I just knew my eyes—isopropyl highball, touch of the old
    hay fever, so called—were drying up forever: vermis aeternum.

Hammer of the Sun

That sound in movies when the lights go on in the football field
  all at once, that thunk that rocks the stadium of night, shudders
alarm across the face of our protagonist, who kneels on turf
  knowing the hand that pulled the switch intends to terrify with this

theatricality of power. It isn't the light per se that scares us here
  but the drastic change in atmosphere, reminding us of how
basic terms of existence can be manipulated so easily, compounded by
  the sudden conspicuousness of one's body on a site designed

for contest and speculation. The message is: we're next, our fate
  sealed on a platform where all outcomes are final. The loud light
watches on in silence now like a god, but one whose cold violet fingers
  sometimes prod a worm of ingenuity to noodle its way through

the interlock of brutal fact—and, after a bit of struggle, set us free.
  Or, more often, not. Circumstances like to be inescapable
and sounds far louder than stadium lights, like the eruption of Krakatoa
  in 1883, so loud it ruptured sailors' eardrums forty miles away,

booming in the Western sky in blood-red floods for months, as echoed
  in Munch's masterpiece, whose central figure feels the "infinite
scream passing through nature" as I do the radioactive laughter of the sun
  drunk on splendor, whose hammer I submit to for as long as it takes.

Further Education

The last mouse left in the experiment has failed to figure out
    the pattern of activity that releases the food pellets
over the course of what seems like a week but is in fact fifteen years,
    far longer than the typical lifespan of a mouse, but of course

many factors are involved, not the least of which is a feeling
    of nausea provoked by the oppressive observation
the mouse is subjected to, and which in turn fills its head
    nonproductively with images of itself from others' perspectives.

Eventually the mouse's longevity earns it a nickname
    among the technicians, but this gets vetoed right away
by members of the board, who know that midstream changes
    might impact the data—in fact, they worry they've already done so.

It doesn't necessarily hurt the mouse to pick it up by its tail,
    but it's not too respectful either, and to my mind the mouse's
refusal to align its behavior to that of other mice or to the expectations
    of science earns it what in layman's terms we call a special place.

When I point this out to the others, they seem not to notice,
    as if I were standing on the distant side of a thick glass wall,
but it's really just a window, and I've been pressing my face
    against it like this all semester, reversing the progress of clouds.

Notes on Flow

The unforthcomingness of basic information, such as what
    we've all been waiting for, whose responsibility it is and what
happens when they fail to perform it, or when they perform it poorly,
    incites a desire rooted in irritation, the kind of itch

that wants answers, its storm surge an echo
    of the mechanism of the aphrodisiac Spanish fly. Tincture of
crushed blister beetles, its active ingredient, cantharidin, when absorbed
    by lipid layers in the epidermis, disrupts transmembrane

proteins that bind cells together, resulting in lesions and pustules.
    I am answering my emails; I am feeling in touch
with the great currents that have guided human striving from the start,
    knowing the domed night sky, uninterrupted, is my backdrop,

and my end point is an arctic pavilion, not some potluck
    in a common space, where everyone apologizes
for misunderstanding one another's tone over plates of murky
    macaroni, which is likewise where I am. Someone compliments

my cupcakes, but speaks ill of me, often, to a colleague. Thanks!
    Must we always live crumbled over so many fronts? What, if I cried out
to anyone in admin, would ever come of it? Nothing, no one, under
    feckless heaven, has time to make good on my beautiful complaint.

Heritage

For the symbolic structures which made sense of the monuments have rotted away . . .
—MARK FISHER

Off to Stonehenge by myself on a coach filled with others,
    couples and families with school-age children, the tour guide
indefatigable as steak and kidney pie, my Marks & Spencer
    chicken vindaloo sandwich nibbled on in the shadows (no food or

drink allowed on board), two canned G&T before a shallow doze
    against the window to the burble of my confreres' deep-cut
Harry Potter trivia, a quick stop in Lacock—idyllic shooting location
    for two out of eight Harry Potter movies and as many episodes

of *Downtown Abbey*, as well as for that series' full-length
    release in which the town's historic streets stand in for those
veining the titular (unreal) village through which George V and Mary
    parade royally in a big-budget set piece featuring 350 extras

in period dress, 80 soldiers on horseback (actual soldiers, the horses
    borrowed from Buckingham Palace's King's Troop), and one
modest royal carriage not wholly incomparable to our own luxury vehicle
    whose claret plush with azure speckles we return to undiminished

by the muchness as we zag through the chilly alkaline grassland
    used for military training now, sundown approaching as we climb
in silence to the stones, where for lack of any better idea we pose
    one by one in front of them like the Night King from *Game of Thrones*.

Mill

AFTER ÉMILE VERHAEREN

Night's turbine is churning very slowly
a heaven of mechanical melancholy,
turning and slowing, its blades the color of leavings,
    sad and weak and tired and heavy, infinitely.

Since morning, pleading, its arms
have reached out and fallen, reached out and fallen
into the soot-black, answerless nothing—
    the unbroken silence of nature extinguished.

Winter sleeps one off on the rooftops,
clouds have started to doubt their integrity,
and past the rampart where snapped cables dangle
    roadways extend toward a lifeless horizon.

Look, over there—ruined dwellings
cluster in a fairy circle; a halogen lamp hangs
from the ceiling in one of them like a gourd, tossing
    its eerie patina on the wall and in the window.

And it's here, in this debris, that we,
night's residents, whose speech you have been
waiting to overhear, have fixed our eyes in silence
    on the turbine as it turns and, powerless, slows and dies.

Wandering Castle

The door kept galloping backwards into the wine-dark wood
  but the music behind it grew louder by the bar and increasingly
out of tune. And what a wake of crushed lady slippers!
  What dazed chanterelles, black aconite and a cultivar of fern

whose shape calls to mind the three-blade titanium propellers
  of our ballyhooed aircraft, all the powerful metaphors
and much fond feeling made possible by the conquest of the air,
  that steadfastness on which to build a nation, an identity!

But the door kept retreating into a cloudbank as voices
  on the other side grew firmer, now adamant, the rudderless
music and rumble of bad dancing long since terminated. No laughter
  ever came of it, but nuts were cracked to illustrate the point.

Only in the lulls between life's peaks did we find any rest,
  lasting always downwards of seven minutes, before the door
struck new ways to evade us, like moving itself onto the stock market
  or splitting off into abstraction, at which point we could hear

pretty much whatever we wanted, and what we wanted was
  the creak of the door as it opened, after which we were no more
shocked to find what came next wasn't cries of valediction but
  galactic silence than we were to discover that the door led out, not in.

Night of the Sound

Night-feeding beetles attracted to lamplight fling their loudness
    up against my window screen repeatedly like the finger of a phantom
lonely to get in. Insect, entity, monster who wants to but doesn't
    quite know how to live, enjoy what you have in this cool coastal air

and gift of flight, the scenic opportunities a night like tonight
    offers creatures small as you, or as semi-invisible, if not entirely.
It takes more than sound to frighten, more than wonder to compel me to
    pull the town car of alone time over and onto the soft shoulder

of the thin road where, just yesterday, solo pedestrian, I nearly
    teetered into cattails stepping aside to let a pickup truck ease by
as I made my way up to the lighthouse close to dusk and it made its way
    back to town. Regaining myself, the wail of a loon

cast its sad amplitude out from the reeds. It is the sound an inter-
    dimensional door makes sliding open. Seconds later, the sought-for reply.
No one lives in the lighthouse anymore, but the granite jetty out front
    juts proudly over two-thousand feet into the harbor, and as I walked it

after dark, I thought of Cocteau's last film, in which he plays a poet
    accused—in a bureaucratic necrosphere—of attempting to trespass into
another world, and how, on soft sand, the bailiff's footsteps sound as if
    he's walking through a ballroom, a soundstage, a mausoleum, right here.

Hush

At night the sea's surface is the penetrable onyx of deep sleep.
    I enter it without fear, as if to lower the input of the eye
reduces risk, and whatever I can't presently see
    exists only in memory, which has been calmed by the water's

cold hypnosis, and to be here is impersonal. Only the moonlight
    interrupts this near-nothingness, the play of it on the glossy swell
like a music you can feel, or like the mapping of something happening to me
    on another level, something that can be understood so long

as it never finishes—and, when it finishes, there is nothing
    left to understand. In the distance, other lights appear now
on the far side of the harbor, and, closer, the dull white gull-like hulls
    of a band of anchored boats rock softly, without intelligence.

Later, elsewhere, I remember it vaguely, and it feels like the most
    meaningful way to go about it, as if the value of it grew
by resisting precision, and that, in coaxing particularity to glide from it
    the sea retained a unity unlike anything other than the sky

with which it had come to merge, but likewise it set itself outside
    the reach of grammar, whose designs on it were not kind, and yet
what I mean by "it" isn't even the sea anymore, but an experience
    of the sea, which syllable by syllable I make the mistake of displacing.

Pink Lotus

It's safe to say that a great painter of seascapes also has to be
    a great painter of the sky, as demonstrated by Lane's canvases
depicting Gloucester Harbor, of which there are many, but one
    in particular makes his aptitude for capturing the evanescence of

the air above water abundantly clear. Here, it's late afternoon
    or early evening, tide low, weedy stones along the shore
just visible through the surface, two fishermen with their backs
    turned to the viewer, one in blue with a fishing pole and the other

lumbering in red, possibly hauling a barrel off, or onto, the rowboat
    hurled up onto, or among, the docks. Exactly when or where or what
everything is and what it's doing isn't as definitive as the overall
    impression, which is of a precariously pale pink hovering over all

the abovementioned, and more: six discernible ships in the harbor,
    others on the horizon, Eastern Point a sliver in the distance
and in the center of it all, but to the left, the tiny Ten Pound Island
    with the lighthouse keeper's dwelling anchored to it like a barnacle

as the light rose haze feathers into an analogous shade of blue
    the way the mind does when a hardship loosens, or in the pause
after long exertion, the heaviness of everything subsiding even slightly
    briefly exciting the pieces of oneself into a single joyous vapor.

Saint Bride

Duncan's angels, whose red-black-pink and gold-green wings
    exceed the margins of the picture plane and inch
out onto the decorative border, carry the sleeping body of the saint
    across the Hebridean sea and back in time to Bethlehem where she

will be Mary's midwife and Christ's wet nurse. Her hands perch
    on her chest in prayer, ghostlier even than the foot
of the angel who flies in front—its face (seen in full) directing our eye
    to the face (in profile) of the saint, its toes likewise dipping

into the trim, which is of gold zigzags, lozenges and dots on a thin
    strip of brown, outlined in madder. Here one impossibility
dances with another, and another, and as decorously as waitstaff
    at La Coupole in Paris, over which the angels might have passed if

they flew to the Nativity via the direct route. My guess is
    they did not. My guess is angels place no premium on efficiency
when trucking in miracles. When I saw the picture in Edinburgh
    I stared for half an hour before gathering the most human face in it

was the seal's, and that it isn't really a seal, but the artist himself
    in seal form, or else how could he have known twin seagulls flew
along in retinue, that angels' tunics are so wickedly emblazoned, or
    which waves that night wove blue-green-blue with little bits of purple?

The Fish Ladder

To be the fish on the ladder
    and not know what it means. To feel the bronzes,
        the pearls, the greens, but in a context
            of pure combat. To fight the literal stream

we hurl ourselves into for no
    discernible purpose, other than some molecule
        says it will be worth it. To feel
            worthless enough to listen. To feel

something rather than nothing—the rungs of it
    a punishment, a goading
        into againstness, against the current. To come to know
            the concrete intimately. To come to know

what we want is. To come to know what we want is
    to be the fish on the ladder
        nonetheless. To feel the sun
            like a god we can discern. We hurl

our self into it, being for this purpose. To come to see
    what there is left to feel. To come to feel
        some other. To come to know
            what we want is. To be the fish on the ladder.

Golden Hour

Too much thought can be given. There can be too much thinking.
    I'm not saying I prefer the alternative. I'm just saying
things start to crack a little under the pressure. The wholeness of them
    bleeds, or it crumbles. So much depends on initial consistency.

I am opening this window all the way. I am lighting a cone of incense
    and burning it down in a quahog's bonelike shell. I am opening
the window on the other wall too. There is cross-ventilation
    and there is silence. The plume from the incense drifts disorganizedly.

Wrong word. It drifts organically. Still not happy. Try again.
    I shut both windows; I shut the door. I place the incense on the floor
and sit beside it perfectly still for three minutes. The plume rises
    straight like a ribbon till it reaches a zone where it starts to ruffle

in a manner my arm hair interprets first as sound, then texture,
    namely of a certain kind of kelp, or of cooked lasagna noodles
but with no hint of dampness, no whiff of the sea, only bergamot, hay,
    and golden poppy—whole plants harvested on bright mornings,

dry loam shaken off the roots, all of it washed at the wash station,
    fanned in the drying room, and taken at last to the lab to be tested
as the plume ascends to the region of chaos, where the beauty of it
    flows in response to a galaxy of variables then vanishes into the ceiling.

The Voices

Falling into a deep lock on the structure of this dahlia, the cinema
 inside my eyes fades to upturned pinecones, tongues of flame, the arches
of a tiny neogothic cathedral organized concentrically
 around a landing pad for bumble bees, and then the wings

of an uninvited presence I can't exactly see, but will compare
 to the figure that stands behind Hesiod in Moreau's watercolor
of that watershed moment the muses climb down from Mount Helicon
 and breathe into the poet "a divine voice to celebrate things."

Its wings, ochre-pink, lift over them both, its face a facsimile
 of Hesiod's own, only much paler, as if the figure were simply
Hesiod himself, but with all the earthly habitudes washed out of him
 (he was a shepherd at the time). Or else maybe it could be

that when a muse visits you, you mirror each other, but with key
 differences, and it's these differences
that make it work—that give it charge, life, lift; propelling you from one
 into infinity. Twice the voices spoke to me, and both times were

not divine, nor celebratory, and pretty much the same, except half of it
 was opposite, but in a way like they knew what they were doing,
so when I dropped the parts that canceled each other out between the first visit
 and the last, the takeaway was yes, they'd help me change the way I feel.

Comfort

Here we drop anchor a minute to consider the classic example
    of a lighthouse keeper—knitted brow, blue wool cap, steady tread
up the winding stair. He is making way to the lantern room
    one last time, whistling a sea tune he has whistled for comfort

a thousand times before. He trims the wick of the whale oil lamp
    and lights it by hand, an act that has always been
literal for him, whereas the rest of us can't stop turning it
    into a metaphor—for hope, guidance, or whatever it might mean

when obscurity reverses, particularly if by the hand
    of one who acts remotely in the interests of a stranger
in the grip of certain peril, no matter that they lack any recognizable
    investment in each other. The nature of it isn't personal any more than light

chooses the surfaces it lands on. And yet, when the light refers
    back to the effort of a person in a tower anonymously
watching over everyone at sea, it's hard not to detect in it a degree
    of abstract human warmth, a property our machinery can't measure

let alone produce—an aroma of care, the gift of a neighborhood
    bakery late at night, such that when our lighthouse keeper wakes
displaced by automation, we sense an incremental loss, first in what it is
    we think we might be made of, then in what we think we're for.

Point Being

Elucidate for me this one last thing, you who I presume
    have been listening all along, here at the seam of what goes without saying
and what goes unsaid—what does it mean
    to be in touch with the largeness when the largeness leaves

no footnotes, no guidelines with respect to
    best practices? Is it up to us to decide what to do
when light ravishes; is it enough just to have stepped outside oneself
    and then back in, and on to whatever errand we were on, shoveling snow

or standing in line for vaccine? I would hate to be that person
    who can't take a gift graciously, who needs to know
exactly what it is and what it's for, instead of admiring its contours
    and the overall gesture, and waiting to get back home before figuring it out.

But, I *am* home. And I don't know where to start. Some days the weight
    of one day after another
occupies my chest like a capybara, and I lie in bed watching
    my in-box lengthen as the rodent stares me down, communicating with me

speechlessly, wanting to know what lunch looks like. So we make a deal
    that I'll make it ramen if it promises to go away. And after I do
and it disappears, I pick up where I left off, but always listening out for
    its webbed feet on my floorboards, sweeping for proof it was ever really here.

Enchantment

A length of utility string appeared out of nowhere, tied in a loop
    and knotted around the curved wooden leg of an antique nightstand
in a small room in a large house I was living in for a time
    rephrasing my thoughts and eating in silence at an empty table.

Years later, under similar circumstances, I revisit the room
    without incident at first, but after a few nights, another loop appears
only this time it's suspended, inexplicably, between the glass
    and the screen of the shut window I have risen from bed to open.

Who knows how long it has been there, collecting what kind of data
    and for what dark purpose? But somehow it moves me.
I had snipped the first string with toiletry scissors, but this time
    I make a video of it hovering there, twisting in night's light breeze.

As I walk into town, silence and imagination arrange the two loops
    into a pair of eyes, which tells me to keep looking, and then
they meld into a single loop, thicker, thickening, a knothole in a fence
    I look through to find only brightness, which gradually focuses

into a figure in a yellow dress, and she is the sun, and she is taking
    laundry down from the line, white sheets, which are the blank pages
of life's enormous calendar, and as she folds them, she lays them
    mathematically in a basket, into the happiness of time bound in space.

To Eat a Peach

One day I won't react when called by name or to the light
    slap on the cheek to break me from the sleep that isn't sleep.
I will be still, and yet I won't. One night my living feet
    will graze the floor like ducks across a pond one final time and lift

off into the dark of anyone's guess. Somewhere a word is
    waiting to be the last I speak. It might be I used it
in passing today. It might be I'm using it now. We know this
    all too well—all things end, and each specifically as this peach

picked at an orchard days ago, skin shaggy as a lagomorph.
    You have to rub it off under cold running water before you'd ever
dream of eating it. In all cases, there's a peach that's closer
    to where you are than all other peaches. Reach out and take it

before what's next. Who's been ripening in a brown paper bag?
    We all have. Isolating, solving for X. I worry the divots
mark places where the flesh has succumbed to catastrophe, but they
    surprise me every time, almost like sunset, or like a wellness

center I enter through my mouth, till I'm right in the middle of
    the last peach of a season thick with peaches—its juice ridiculous
in rivers down my chin, liturgy of almond pushed through plush
    walls of mango—and in the heaven of it, I don't even know who I am.

Bóín Dé

Little cow of god, the wattage of your red
    reverberates the earth, and spots of onyx nestle
on its lacquer like fixed stars. Bravissima! You are red's
    least loud-mouthed ambassador, paradise's minuscule half-apple

mobilized by a half dozen legs, and under
    the split-open dome of you: gold-leaf wings, folded over
esoterically, like dress patterns, whose thinness whispers to the near-
    devotional care called for to pin them out properly.

Meanwhile, your antennae, animate, demonstrate
    sensitivity with a nonchalance that shames the bureaucrat.
Thanks for that! You serve purpose in the garden, but at the moment
    what matters is I see you . . .

Little cow of god, who had been sleeping on a pom-pom
    I sewed by hand onto a store-bought curtain till I jostled you
awake, you who flew to my laptop's light and landed on the staves of
    my worksurface, tell me—am I dying?

Little cow, blood-drop omen, stopped in front of me like a whole
    note in a chorus that celebrates the invisible
labor of useless thought—you who had grown tired, I have grown
    old, but is it over, our irrelevant haven, this thimble's worth of song?

Chariot (I)

Confusion of the verb *to chair*, meaning to accommodate
    both bodily and otherwise, as in "The buttercup's bright chalice
chairs the morning dew," or "How much more of this do you
    suppose the heart can chair," which is a question apt to throw

a person off at first, who envisions a throne, likely of gold-
    leafed wood, thrown into the heart's red blaze—iconographic,
cartoonish, and soon to combust—as is the heart, the other
    counters, at last understood. Alone, I cupped my palms to chair

tadpoles as a boy, a jar did after that, and then the pond
    chaired them back again and into frog adulthood
over time, which chairs the total of what is, pulling us along
    in its procession like a chariot, irreversibly deeper into itself

and likewise across space, as if a jumble of chalk horses
    on ascent into cerulean, azure, aquamarine—all the blues
Redon used late in life after decades of lithographs and charcoals.
    How did we get here? Unclear, if it matters; what matters

is we stay—aloft in possible color, all the oil paints and pastels
    that came to represent for the painter "a reconciliation
with the external world," as I just now read in a book, which is
    a vessel to chair the world, itself a vessel to chair all possible books.

Chariot (II)

Mark Antony broke
    lions to the yoke, and was the first Roman to harness them
to a chariot. He did this to demonstrate how even the most valorous
    hearts can be bent

into service. His enemies
    got the message. As for me, I don't like to see points made
as brutally as that, or our metaphors bound so tight, that entities that might
    animate each other

perpetually, in radiant
    transport (and not just enemies and lions anymore, but anything
we have a word for—amphitheaters, antibodies, happiness, icebergs, loss),
    end up instead

bound by force, flattening
    being into deathlike stasis. As I write, I don't want to be dead
any more than I want to see the breathing flower of our language suffer
    into service, but I know

as well as anyone
    that's the nature of it. And yet, moving forward, if another sentence
follows on the heels, as this one does, I say that when it ends, its ending will
    unharness lions.

This Is the Assemblage

speaking. Do you read me? We have been waiting for you here
    in the shadow of our metaphor, under the seats of this thunderous
theater, on a hacienda loud with parakeets, which is itself
    an assemblage of assemblages. You can see how there is no

end to this. Times like these we are immortal together. Say the word
    and you're our conqueror. Find the treasure and we split it
like an atom. Find the portal and we'll take it like a daytrip, a trope,
    a paratrooper at the bomb bay door. We are what we are, only

infinitely better: old-school, ostensible, and not all that hiding
    stuff up our sleeves—it's just arms and arms, which we admit to
freely. They extend to meet your needs. And how they keep you
    company: like a burgundy you can attune yourself to accordingly,

sip after sip. Golden apple, yellow pear. We are not worthless
    here, but cradled in a hold the escape from which is ever-imminent
even after it happens, even when we stand for nothing in particular
    other than the motion of it. More than furniture, more than vehicle

with wheels or wings, we are the voice you choose when you can't
    choose two. We are your portion of all things. So if you feel as if
a spell is cast on you, or you can't quite account for yourself, remember
    we'll always be here at the bottom of it, over. All we have is life.

Notes

SEA WHISTLE refers to Théodore Géricault's *The Raft of the Medusa* (1819).

NIGHT OF THE MARIGOLDS refers to Eugène Delacroix's *Horse Frightened by a Storm* (1824).

ELEVATION, ALL VANISHES, EGLANTINE, and MILL are freely translated from the French of Charles Baudelaire, Comte de Lautréamont, Marceline Desbordes-Valmore, and Émile Verhaeren, respectively.

THE YELLOW BOAT, ANGEL OF THE HEARTH, NOCTURNE, THE COWS, HEAD OF ORPHEUS, and SAINT BRIDE pay homage to, and take their titles from, paintings by Pierre Bonnard, Max Ernst, James Abbott McNeill Whistler, Vincent van Gogh, Odilon Redon, and John Duncan, respectively.

SUMMERHEAD quotes Plutarch as cited in Dudley Wright's *The Eleusinian Mysteries and Rites* (1913). The poem's title is taken from the 1993 song by the Cocteau Twins.

ETRUSCAN VASE WITH FLOWERS adapts a line from Donald Cammell's film *Demon Seed* (1977, screenplay by Robert Jaffe and Roger O. Hirson), as well as from Odilon Redon's *To Myself* (1922), translated by Mira Jacob and Jeanne L. Wasserman. The poem's title is taken from a painting by Redon.

DRIFT adapts a sentence from Nietzsche's *Human, All Too Human* (1878), translated by R. J. Hollingdale.

MYTH is adapted from "Huntings and Enchantments," chapter x, "The Shadowy One," in Lady Augusta Gregory's *Gods and Fighting Men* (1904).

THE BARD OF ARMAGH takes its rhymes from the nineteenth-century English translation of the late seventeenth-century Irish ballad of the same name attributed to Bishop Patrick Donnelly.

BEAUPORT is in homage to the Sleeper-McCann House in Gloucester, Massachusetts.

MAULED BY DOGS refers to Georges Franju's film *Eyes Without a Face* (1960).

NIGHT OF THE EARWORM cites the lyrics to "It's All Coming Back to Me Now" (1989), written by Jim Steinman.

HAMMER OF THE SUN cites Edvard Munch's diary entry dated January 22, 1892 and alludes to his painting *The Scream* (1893).

DIGGING FOR APPLES takes its title from Lewis Carroll's *Alice's Adventures in Wonderland* (1865).

WANDERING CASTLE takes its title from Paul Éluard's essay "Poetry's Evidence" (1932).

NIGHT OF THE SOUND refers to Jean Cocteau's film *Testament of Orpheus* (1960).

PINK LOTUS is in homage to Fitz Henry Lane's *Ten Pound Island* (1850s).

Acknowledgments

I am indebted and deeply grateful to everyone who read and commented on this book in manuscript, namely Mary Jo Bang, Julia Burgdorff, Alan Gilbert, Binnie Kirshenbaum, Brett Fletcher Lauer, and Elizabeth Metzger.

I am likewise indebted and grateful to everyone at Wave Books and to friends, colleagues, students, and family who supported and inspired me while writing these poems, especially my parents and daughters, and above all Lynn Melnick, whose love and wisdom have transported me through decades.

Lastly, I am grateful to the T. S. Eliot Foundation and everyone at the T. S. Eliot House, where many of these poems were written and a vision of this book was first conceived, as well as to the editors of the following publications in which these poems first appeared:

32 Poems: "Night of the MacGuffin," "No Small Task"

American Poetry Review: "Drift," "Excelsior," "The Fish Ladder," "In My Life," "Point Being"

The Baffler: "Further Education"

Bennington Review: "A Page from the Weather," "This Is the Assemblage"

The Best American Poetry 2023: "Instagram"

The Brooklyn Review: "The Cows"

Colorado Review: "Digging for Apples," "The Yellow Boat"

Conduit: "The Gist of It," "Likely Story"

Conjunctions: "Angel of the Hearth," "Chariot (I)," "Nocturne," "Ultramarine," "Where Space Begins"

The Daily Telegraph: "Night of Embodiment"

Denver Quarterly: "Home at Last"

The Drift: "Bóin Dé"

Fence: "Honeymouth," "Reality Hit Me"

The Hopkins Review: "Notes on Flow," "Vantablack"

Image: "Boom," "Comfort," "Summerhead"

Laurel Review: "Golden Hour," "Mauled by Dogs," "Sea Whistle"

The Nation: "The Light"

The New Republic: "Nothing Happened"

The New Yorker: "Head of Orpheus," "Hush"

Oversound: "Myth," "Night of the Earworm," "What It Is About People"

Plume: "Etruscan Vase with Flowers," "Instagram"

Poetry: "Elevation"

Prairie Schooner: "Not Much More to It Than That"

A Public Space: "Hammer of the Sun," "Night of the Marigolds"

Southern Humanities Review: "The Voices"

Together in a Sudden Strangeness: America's Poets Respond to the Pandemic:
    "Weather Heard as Music"

Washington Square Review: "Domesticity"

The Yale Review: "Night of the Gowanus," "Night of Oblivion"